The Pocket Apostle

By

Chuck Sullivan

Published by David McKay Publication
First Edition
Printed in the United States of America
ISBN
Paperback: 979-8-90321-060-2
For permissions, media inquiries, or bulk purchase information,
please contact:
info@davidmckaypublication.com

Table of Contents

DEDICATION

Dedicated to all the non-believers who have been scorned by the religious;

All the religious believers who have scorned their fellow man,

And anyone who is searching for the truth.

ARE YOU THERE?

Over the past several years, I have heard a number of people make comments to the effect that something feels different, that something is off. They do not know what it is, only that it gives them an expectant feeling of something more than what they currently understand. A longing you could say from the farthest depths, a light in the darkness. A primal scream emanating from the inner man. Could it be that we are in a season of enlightenment and everyone can feel it? Some call it the Great Awakening, while others label it as the Great Reset. Some plan for a day of freedom while others plan for a day of enslavement. Some hoard gold so that they may have something to trade, while others stockpile weapons so that they may hold their position in the face of what is to come. All the while, people of each kind fall to their knees to pray to God or to whichever gods they hold contract with; so that they may be delivered from tomorrow.

The common thread is predominantly this: that there is a piece that is missing, an intangible understanding that is needed to transcend the madness that surrounds us. We are willing to subject ourselves to any pursuit that may bring truth into an otherwise deceitful world. There are many gnostic avenues, many of which are mirrored by mankind's New Age religions. Many seek the security of human understanding— follow the science to the grave—seeking knowledge from men who crave accolades before understanding, to be elevated in their wisdom, for whatever that may be worth.

Many have tried going to church but are quickly turned off by the self-righteousness of the typical congregation—followers of Christ who do not reflect the heart of Jesus, shedding darkness on the truth that they themselves do not understand. We can't expect someone new to church to pick up on the differences through the deception at work. We are taught to evaluate what is seen, and when someone sees hypocrisy or judgment, the soul is lost to continue their search for the missing piece in their lives.

My desire for this writing is that it will open the eyes of the deceived. I share information that was revealed to me as understanding from Him, through prayer and the Word—that a person can be alone but still grow with God, still be trained spiritually in the truth. There is nothing wrong with good teachers, but your personal relationship with Jesus is the only rock to build on. You will read that understanding does not come from man but directly from God.

So my revelation—which to anyone else is only information—can put you on the path to firsthand knowledge of the Truth and the wonder of enlightenment through Jesus Christ. I pray that each and every one of you experiences it.

BRIEF TESTIMONY

My family attended church throughout my childhood—a small, non-denominational gospel church full of God-fearing country people. I thought all churches were of this mold: repentant, obedient, direct representatives of Jesus. A loving body with one motive: to further the kingdom of heaven. The veil of innocence would soon be torn.

When I was around twelve, I started attending a Wednesday night youth program at the First Baptist Church in town. Several of my friends from school attended. We would hang out and shoot hoops for an hour, then have our Bible study. That lasted a couple of years, until one day I inquired about membership in the church. See, all of my friends were members, and I only lived a block away—this will be perfect! My youth pastor set up a meeting with an under-shepherd so that I understood the process. I was full of excitement; the interview was going well—this could be a new page of growing in Christ.

"Young man, are you saved and baptized?"

"Yes, sir."

"Through what kind of church? Was it a Baptist church?"

"No, sir—Old Time Gospel."

"Well, son, you will have to be saved again in our church to become a member, but I don't see any problems beyond that."

"But sir, my preacher is a good man, a man of God who teaches the Word. I've known him my whole life. Are you saying his work is no good?"

Even at fourteen years old, I understood that something was not right.

"Look, I'm sure he's a fine man," continued the under-shepherd, "but if you want to be a member of this church, you have to be saved in this church."

I never returned to that church or set foot on campus. I knew in my heart that something wasn't right.

Religion is a scam! Religion is a lie!

So that means Jesus is a lie!

See, as a child, I failed to realize that religion and Jesus are not one and the same—that religion is theology through the understanding of man, built by man for man's motives. Jesus is the truth, and no man is needed for us to come into a relationship with Christ.

I spent the next thirty-five years railing against the evils of organized religion, the congregations that preached one thing and lived another. Fueled by Texas pride, rebellious anger, and my limited understanding, I was turned over to darkness, where I would be thoroughly sifted.

By trade, I was a carpenter, songwriter, and whiskey connoisseur. We bought a place in the hills of the Ozarks, away from everyone and surrounded by forests—a place where peace and understanding may be had. I was closer to contentment but still away from God. What I know now is that He was putting me in a place so that when He got my attention, He would keep it.

I had spent many years chasing lies in hopes of finding truth—human nature, I guess, to be easily deceived and easily distracted.

Then came the pivot: a debilitating stem stroke. In one moment, out went the carpentry and guitar playing. I lost my taste for drink. Nothing was the same and never would be again.

This was the Lord bringing me to my knees. This was the beginning of understanding mysteries through teachings and revelations straight from Jesus, through the Holy Spirit.

SPIRITUAL WARFARE

The greatest trick of the devil is convincing the world that he never existed. If he is written off as folklore or superstition, then all the better. He can go about his schemes largely unnoticed, devouring everything in his path, leaving a trail of anger and ruin—of desolation without hope. The flesh is an easy play for him; he has had since the beginning to refine his deceptions.

1 Peter 5:8

Be of sober spirit, be on the alert. Your adversary, the devil, prowls about like a roaring lion, seeking someone to devour.

We must have a basic understanding of spiritual warfare.

This topic, scoffed at by many and generally misunderstood, can bring much ridicule and debate. I bring no debate to the table, for I am not searching for the conspiracy of man; I only seek the truth from Jesus, so that I may avoid the darkness that tends to manifest from argument and needless discussion. My hope is to share the understanding that was imparted to me as information to you, so that a seed may be sown in you, so that you may put yourself on the path that brings you before the wisdom of God. Whether this concept of spiritual warfare fits into your worldview or not is quite irrelevant, considering the reality in which we live.

The rhythm of the world naturally flows in a way contrary to the truth because the world is contrary to God. The world is contrary to God because of angelic rebellions that led to deception. In this deception, the adversary gained legal right to darken humanity.

Isaiah 14:12–15

(12) "How you have fallen from heaven, O star of the morning, son of the dawn! You have been cut down to the earth; you have weakened the nations!"

(13) "But you said in your heart, 'I will ascend to heaven; I will raise my throne above the stars of God, and I will sit on the mount of assembly in the recesses of the north.'

(14) 'I will ascend above the heights of the clouds; I will make myself like the Most High.'"

(15) "Nevertheless, you will be thrust down to Sheol, to the recesses of the pit."

Just as a point of reference, angelic rebellions can be found in Genesis chapter 3—the serpent and Eve, the original fall of man—and Genesis chapter 6, the fall of the sons of God, as it is written in Genesis and also known as the fall of the Watchers, as written in Enoch. This event spawned the Nephilim giants and led to the polytheistic beliefs of ancient religions and many of the little "g" gods of the Bible. Understand that these gods were demonic spirits masquerading as deities to separate man from God. Baal, Molech, and

Asherah are a few of the Semitic dead gods found in the Bible.

If we remember our mythology studies in school, Zeus was the Greek god that the Romans called Jupiter; Poseidon was also known as Neptune, Aphrodite as Venus. Hermes Trismegistus was a combination of the Greek god Hermes and the Egyptian god Thoth. My point being that our minds should consider the fact that ancient mythologies blended with one another across cultures and time.

The Bible is questioned on this very basis—that it took stories from other cultures and is a blending of ideas to create a separate theology. Let me ask you this: where are those gods now? They were lost to history after they destroyed the civilizations that worshiped them. They were lost because they never had true power—underling beings posing as supreme and taking credit for God's work. If it were indeed their own work, why would they destroy it? How could they create with the heart of destruction?

They survived from the fear and the blood of those who followed them. When the blood ran out, and the last child was sacrificed, their time was up. The spirits are still on the earth; they have taken other forms or are working different schemes, but they are still here. Enoch 15 speaks on the origins of demons and the Watchers who are bound until judgment, but the spirits of their soulless offspring will be known as evil spirits on the earth.

Genesis chapter 11, the Tower of Babel—when God went down to confuse the language, in verse seven He says, "Come, let us go down…"

In **Deuteronomy 32:8 (NRSV),** it says that He fixed the boundaries of the people according to the number of gods. He divided the earth into seventy nations. That His own portion was His people; Jacob was His allotment. Not all of these ruling princes remained righteous—many rebelled. The traits of the prince will either bless or curse the principality, and those living in the land will have those traits manifested in their lives.

You will see momentarily the scripture **Ephesians 6:12**, that our fight is not with the flesh but against princes, principalities, powers, rulers of darkness, and wicked spiritual forces in the heavens. Even in the face of all this wickedness, YHWH remains unchallenged, for He is the one true God. He is the only being of His kind. Omnipresence is unique to Him. God is quantum—everywhere at once, through all points in time, through all things in the universe—for all things were created by Him. It is as if God is entangled in everything.

Just because we lack understanding or simply do not believe in what we cannot see does not mean that we are unaffected by the warfare that is all around us—the warfare that is in us this very minute. In fact, disbelief will ensure that you will fall victim to the deception. Would the layman who does not understand the nuances of mass manipulation be any less manipulated? Would he not be all the more deceived? Will he who is determined to be defined by man ever know truth, or only understand the sting of death?

2 Corinthians 4:18

While we look not at the things which are seen but at the things which are not seen; for the things that are seen are temporary, but the things that are not seen are eternal.

Paul is very cut and dry in this verse. There are two realms: one we see and one we do not. One is eternal, while the other is not. If there are two realms, why would we limit ourselves to the understanding of the lesser? It is clear that there is acknowledgment throughout society and through the entirety of the history of man—from modern-day stories of spooks and orbs to haunted history tales of curses from the undead. We have an unlimited amount of supernatural media which confirms our general belief that, as a whole, we know that there is something more than what is seen.

We live in the realm of the flesh—worldly, temporary, enslaved, under attack, and deceived. Those who are in the realm of the flesh cannot please God **(Romans 8:8)**. Pay attention to the results of the actions of people and groups. If they produce anger, confusion, division, or negative emotions, then these are fruits of the flesh. When you see positive emotions—love, joy, peace, and the like—these are fruits of the Spirit. It is much like the age-old analogy of a devil on one shoulder and an angel on the other: classic good versus evil. It is mostly cut and dry—one side or the other.

The tools and understanding needed to overcome darkness are lacking because they are hidden. The world keeps us distracted through relentless stimulation, unending noise, and a constant bombardment that makes it very easy to miss God when He speaks. The devil also masquerades as a being of light. He is the prince of the airwaves, the master of deception. Is it any surprise that you feel beaten and bruised—overwhelmed and ready to crack? This is the life of one who has lost the path to peace, who has no protection against the insanity—the natural man lost in the world. Do not fear, for this is not the end, but you already knew that.

1 John 4:4

"You are from God, little children, and have overcome them; because greater is He that is in you than he that is in the world."

Romans 8:6

"For the mind set on the flesh is death, but the mind set on the Spirit is life and peace."

The Holy Spirit gives us access to this realm, and our walk in the Spirit gives us access to the Father. This is where we must be to receive understanding and revelation.

"You are not in the flesh but in the Spirit, if indeed the Spirit of God dwells in you."

2 Corinthians 10:3–5

(3) For though we walk in the flesh, we do not war according to the flesh.

(4) For the weapons of our warfare are not of the flesh but mighty in God for pulling down strongholds,

(5)Casting down arguments and every high thing that exalts itself against the knowledge of God, bringing every thought into captivity to the obedience of Christ.It appears that a line has been drawn in the sand. There is a lot going on that we cannot understand without revelation from Him. Without His understanding, our eternal spirit will be lost through the deception of our mind and the hardening of our heart.

John 16:33

"These things I have spoken to you, so that in Me you may have peace. In the world you have tribulation, but take courage; I have overcome the world."

Let us end this chapter with a passage on how to defend ourselves from the adversary, to be prepared and ready.

Ephesians 6:11–18

(11) Put on the full armor of God, that you may be able to stand firm against the schemes of the devil.

(12) For our struggle is not against flesh and blood, but against the rulers (principalities), against the powers, against the world forces of this darkness, against the spiritual forces of wickedness in the heavenly places.

(13) Therefore, take up the full armor of God, that you may be able to resist in the evil day, and having done everything, to stand firm.

(14) Stand firm therefore, having girded your loins with truth, and having put on the breastplate of righteousness.

(15) And having shod your feet with the preparation of the gospel of peace.

(16) In addition to all, take up the shield of faith, with which you will be able to extinguish all the flaming missiles of the evil one.

(17) And take the helmet of salvation, and the sword of the Spirit, which is the Word of God.

(18) With all prayer and petition, pray at all times in the Spirit, and with this in view, be on the alert with all perseverance and petition for all the saints.

FAITH AND FRUITS

2 Corinthians 5:7

"For we walk by faith, not by sight."

Many may argue that there is no faith in them or that they could never find the faith to put into God. Rest easy, my friend, for it is already inside of us. **Romans 12:3** states that God has allotted to each (man) a measure of faith. Faith is the key that unlocks answers to questions which have been long sought after and the understanding of mysteries largely unsolved.

Matthew 17:19–20

(19) Then the disciples came to Jesus privately and said, "Why were we not able to cast them out?"

(20) And He said to them, "Because of the littleness of your faith; for truly I say to you, if you have faith as a mustard seed, you shall say to this mountain, 'Move from here to there,' and it shall move; and nothing shall be impossible to you."

He can take a very small amount of faith, for mustard seeds are very small indeed, and transform the mind of the person who walks in the Holy Spirit. This leads to the purification of the heart. Through this process of repentance, obedience, and refinement, we transform into our new identity in Him.

It is a communion of exchange—He is a loving Father with gifts. Anything we give to Him, we will receive something back. We give up our hate, He will give us joy. We give up our drunkenness, He will give us self-control. If we give up our idols, He gives us dominion and the understanding of the true power of Him who is inside us. Ask Him for your faith to be strengthened, and He will burn away the guilt and the regret. He will turn your past trauma into gentleness through revelation—a process that will become more and more evident as you turn away from the desires of the flesh.

Now that we have laid a bit of groundwork, let us dive into the process and discuss some key points that are necessary in developing our relationship in Christ.

Jesus nailed the flesh to the cross so that the sins of our flesh would be covered by His sacrifice. Through this, we receive the free gift of grace, so that the debt of sin, which is death, has been taken from us. So that we may have the ears to hear the knowledge that salvation is needed, and the eyes to see the path of purification. So that we may rise out of the darkness through the process of transformation, in which, in His fullness, we have received grace upon grace for our protection throughout our refinement. So that we may throw off the chains of enslavement and abide in love and peace.

Every spirit that confesses that Jesus Christ has come in the flesh is of God, and every spirit that does not confess that Jesus Christ has come in the flesh is not from God.

1 John 4:2–3

Many will ask for a sign to establish their faith. The Greek mindset that we are taught in school assumes that existence requires proof through scientific observation. Without the opportunity to witness the creation of our existence, we sift through physical layers, man embracing the burden of proof alone. Despite centuries of research by our most celebrated scholars—accepting, disputing, presenting theories and speculations—we are no closer to any form of tangible knowledge that resembles actual understanding.

At some point, common sense dictates that we should be receptive to intangible proofs that will always be outside of our vision, just beyond our scope. Once we find ourselves on the correct path, then we will start to see growth in our physical knowledge. Let us not misplace our faith in man's theories. Let us not be deceived when they are presented to us as truth.

1 Corinthians 1:22

"For indeed, Jews ask for signs and Greeks search for wisdom."

When I put my faith in Him, when I started in the Word, when I began my prayer life, only then did I start to receive signs from Him—nuggets of understanding that He uses to grow and strengthen our faith. We apply faith, prayer, and obedience, and He shares love, understanding, and peace. With perseverance, through whatever tests the world may have, He will give you truths beyond the understanding of the natural man.

Everyone seeks enlightenment; you could say it is primal, flowing through each individual. Understand—it feels universal because each individual carries in us He who created us, YHWH.

Most of the information I am sharing with you comes from the teachings of the letters of Paul. You can find his commission in **Acts chapter 9**. Paul's understanding was achieved through revelations that came directly from Christ. In his teachings are found the secrets to the flesh and spirit, worldly relationships and relationships with Christ, what we see, what we do not see—the keys to the truth. Through his teachings, we are given the path to walking in the Spirit and receiving lessons that bring us into a personal bond with Jesus Christ. From this point, the teachings of Jesus come alive, and Biblical understanding is more accessible.

Galatians 1:12 Paul writes,"For I neither received it from man, nor was I taught it, but

I received it through a revelation of Jesus Christ."

Many are confused on where our understanding comes from. There are many good teachers, good preachers, good churches, and good media that can give us more information than can be consumed. That comes from a good place, but true understanding comes from Him.

Proverbs 3:5

"Trust in the Lord with all your heart and do not lean on your own understanding."

What help can it be to lean on another's understanding when they are advised not to lean on it themselves? This is a trick the devil uses throughout society, most visible in our educational institutions and in our denominational worship buildings.

Take any information given to you straight to Christ. He will make your paths straight through the understanding of the truth. Through prayer, through the Bible, through your determination to walk in obedience, to keep the darkness of the world from consuming your mind and infecting your heart—through these things we are better positioned to grow in Christ and to receive the spiritual gifts and understanding He promises.

Here, Paul is speaking of himself and Apollos, both as preachers in the early church.

1 Corinthians 3:6

"I planted, Apollos watered, but God caused the growth."

Man can plant the seed, man can water the plant, but it is not the power of man that makes the plant grow. It is God that does the work.

How can we tell what information is good or bad? What is from the Holy Spirit and what is from the spirit of antichrist? How do we know if someone's motives are good? How do we know if our motives are good? We know these things through the gift of discernment.

When we are in relationship with Christ, all we must do is ask (spiritual requests, not desires of the flesh). He loves to teach us, to give us what we need to overcome the world.

When I realized that He wants us to ask for spiritual gifts so that we may have what we need to rise above the schemes of the adversary, I prayed for discernment and understanding, patience, and wisdom. We have got to be able to spot a fake from the genuine article and then know how to proceed according to His will. So the first place He points me is **Galatians** and **Philippians**. Let us dive into the fruits, which can be thought of as actions, results, motives, or source, be it of truth or of lies.

For the flesh sets its desire against the Spirit, and the Spirit against the flesh, for these are in opposition to one another.

Galatians 5:19–21 (of the flesh)

(19) Now the deeds of the flesh are evident, which are: immorality, impurity, sensuality,

(20) idolatry, sorcery, enmities, strife, jealousy, outbursts of anger, disputes, dissensions, factions,

(21) envying, drunkenness, carousing, and things like these, of which I have forewarned you, that those who practice such things shall not inherit the kingdom of God.

Galatians 5:22–23 (of the Spirit)

(22) But the fruit of the Spirit is love, joy, peace, patience, kindness, goodness, faithfulness;

(23) gentleness, self-control; against such things there is no law.

If you are unsure about your thoughts, someone else's thoughts, your plan or the plans of another, your actions or the actions of an individual or group, then run it through these verses. See how it lines up. Now we are developing discernment. Keep in mind that just because we discern darkness in others does not necessarily mean that they are the devil incarnate. Maybe they are going through refinement in their lives; maybe they are being sifted. These are not things for us to dwell on, for if we dwell on the darkness of others, then we can fill ourselves with darkness. Pray that His will be done.

Through discernment we become aware of truths and lies, the light and darkness in our surroundings, as well as within ourselves. Now we have a starting point to pray for renewal and refinement. Are we seeing anger, pride, worry, or unforgiveness? Jealousy, turmoil, unhealthy lusts for carnal pleasure? These things are of the world, and we have to give them to Jesus. He will give you understanding in exchange for these old habits. He is the path to overcome the darkness. We must be self-aware so that we may see the issues that need to be addressed and humble enough to realize that we cannot overcome the world without Him.

Take it to the Lord in prayer.

Always pray in the spirit of thanksgiving and appreciation. Incline your heart to Him. Ask for discernment and understanding. Pray for self-control and wisdom. Our salvation is not a cookie-cutter, one-size-fits-all situation as far as what He calls us to do. We each have our own purpose in His plan: preaching, teaching, administration, deliverance, healing. Pray for any gifts that are needed to carry out His will for you. There are many people and groups that desperately want to fill the world with peace. Jesus **IS** peace. It cannot be done on our own, but only through individual transformation through Him may we bring the true power of love into the world.

James 1:5

"But if any of you lacks wisdom, let him ask of God, who gives to all men generously and without reproach, and it will be given to him."

Let me end our discussion on fruits with a note I found in Grandpa's Bible; he said, "Dwell on these things." I feel like it is a perfect complement to the verses in **Galatians 5**, and it does well to lead us into the topics of controlling fleshly emotions and desires.

Philippians 4:6–9

(6) Be anxious for nothing, but in everything by prayer and supplication with thanksgiving, let your request be made known to God.

(7) And the peace of God, which surpasses all comprehension, shall guard your hearts and your minds in Christ Jesus.

(8) Finally, brethren, whatever is true, whatever is honorable, whatever is right, whatever is pure, whatever is lovely, whatever is of good repute, if there is any excellence and if anything worthy of praise, let your mind dwell on these things.

(9) The things you have learned and received and heard and seen in me, practice these things, and the God of peace shall be with you.

CHRIST IN YOU: ACCEPTANCE AND SURRENDER

Acts 4:12

"And there is salvation in no one else; for there is no other name under heaven that has been given among men, by which we must be saved."

How can we hear from Christ if we do not follow Him? How can He have access to those who do not acknowledge Him? How can this internal calling be felt by a non-believer?

Isaiah 45:18

"For thus says the Lord, Who created the heavens, Who is God, Who did not create it in vain, Who formed it to be inhabited: 'I am the Lord; and there is no other.'"

He created all the heavens and all the earth — the angels and man; every being there is subject to Him. He has dominion as the Creator, and through that He can access any of His creation.

I know, I know — bring on the dying screams of evolutionary theory, old Earth and new Earth debates, ancient aliens and civilizations of old, differing creation stories, the chicken or the egg, and all deceptions under the sun. There is nothing new; the same old tricks and lies have been used by the adversary since the ages before us. At some point, we must open our minds to see beyond human understanding.

Christ lives in us through the Holy Spirit. He stands at the door of the unbeliever in love, hoping that one day His knock will be answered and His truth revealed.

We are asked to nurture this relationship through the Word, prayer, and obedience. If we do this with faith and a daily desire to renew our minds in the Holy Spirit — who is

Christ in us — then we are rewarded with teachings, revelations, deeper understanding, and wisdom. Most of all, the renewing of the mind leads to a pure heart.

God's will is free will. Everyone has the choice to open the door. We can put our faith in Christ and seek the truth, or we can put our faith in the world and remain in deception.

A personal relationship with Jesus is the narrow road to salvation, and without it, He will say, *"I never knew you."*

The initial step is accepting Jesus Christ as your personal Savior. This requires an investment of faith—faith in the truth that we are saved by His grace, which is sufficient for us **(2 Corinthians 12:9)**. God's grace brings us to a place where we can see our brokenness and strengthens us to walk in the Spirit, allowing us to be unburdened by our sin and the worldly emotions that come with it.

We learn to shed the strongholds of the past and build peace for the future. This process takes time and perseverance. There will be seasons when you feel alone, but know this: He is at work in you. If you are suffering, it is part of the growing pains—a path to removing pride, anger, unforgiveness, and regret. Keep your eyes on Him, and the things of the world will burn away.

John 14:6

"Jesus said unto him, 'I am the way, and the truth, and the life; no one comes to the Father, but through Me.'"

This is not religion but relationship. We must understand that God sent Jesus to die for our sins, and in this sacrifice, we are forgiven, freed from the bondage of Satan, and given a path to salvation.

We must believe: the foundation of accepting Christ is faith that He is who He says He is.

We must acknowledge our sin (**Romans 3:23**).

We must believe that Jesus' sacrifice on the cross paid the penalty for our sins, and through His death we are forgiven (**John 3:16**).

We must confess our sins to Him through prayer and repent of the sinful ways of our flesh (**Acts 3:19; Romans 10:9–10**).

(9) "That if you confess with your mouth Jesus as Lord, and believe in your heart that God raised Him from the dead, you will be saved.

(10) "For with the heart a person believes, resulting in righteousness, and with the mouth he confesses, resulting in salvation."

In the simplest of terms, you can pray a heartfelt prayer, thankful for the gift you are about to receive, God's grace, and all the blessings that come with it:

Dear Heavenly Father,

I know that I am a sinner, and I ask for Your forgiveness.

I believe You died for my sins and rose from the dead.

I turn from my sins; I repent of my sins.

I invite You to come into my heart and life.

I want to trust and follow You as my Lord and Savior.

In Jesus' name, Amen.

He is alive! I have given my life not to a dead Christ, but to a living Christ!

He has given me a song to sing, a flag to follow.

I have reason for existence; I know where I have come from, I know why I am here, and I know where I am going. Do you? — *Billy Graham*

2 Corinthians 13:5-6

(5) "Examine yourselves as to whether you are in the faith. Test yourselves. Do you not know yourselves that Jesus Christ is in you? Unless indeed you are disqualified."

(6) "But I trust that you will know that we are not disqualified."

Now we can stand on solid ground, strengthened by the fact that we are, without doubt, qualified.

Let us walk in repentance, searching the Word daily for knowledge that will be turned into understanding, wisdom, and discernment through daily prayer and communion with the Spirit of Christ in us.

Galatians 2:20

"I have been crucified with Christ; it is no longer I who live, but Christ lives in me; and the life which I now live in the flesh, I live by faith in the Son of God, who loved me and gave Himself for me."

Colossians 1:27

"To them God willed to make known what are the riches of the glory of this mystery among the Gentiles: which is Christ in you, the hope of glory."

Ephesians 3:14-18

(14) "For this reason I bow my knees to the Father of our Lord Jesus Christ,

(15) from whom the whole family in heaven and on Earth is named,

(16) that He would grant you, according to the riches of His glory, to be strengthened with might through His Spirit in the inner man,

(17) that Christ may dwell in your hearts through FAITH; that you, being rooted and grounded in love,

(18) may be able to comprehend with all the saints what is the length, width, breadth, and height."

If we invite Him into our hearts, He will teach us the mysteries for which we have no worldly answers. Through the gifts of grace and love, He teaches us the way to peace. By giving us eyes to see and ears to hear, we gain discernment in how to view the world. We grow to understanding that the Renewal of the mind leads to the wisdom to overcome the darkness that fights to overwhelm us.

John 14:23

"Jesus answered and said to him, 'If anyone loves Me, he will keep My word, and My Father will love him, and We will come to him and make our abode with him.'"

THE NEW SELF AND WALKING IN OBEDIENCE

2 Corinthians 5:17

"Therefore, if anyone is in Christ, he is a new creature; the old things have passed away; behold, new things have come."

Ephesians 4:22-24

(22) "That, in reference to your former manner of life, you lay aside the old self, which is being corrupted in accordance with the lusts of deceit,

(23) and that you be renewed in the spirit of your mind,

(24) and put on the new self, which in the likeness of God has been created in righteousness and holiness of the truth."

Now that we have accepted Him into our life so that we may know the truth of grace, and can begin wrapping our minds around working out our salvation, we can step into the new self in Jesus. Having crucified our old self with Him in repentance, we set aside our old ways. Now we must establish our repentance through daily obedience.

Our minds are hard-wired to the patterns of the world. We must train our minds to follow the ways of the Lord. This is the process of refinement and spiritual training: letting go of old darkness and embracing the light we now receive.

We approach this new relationship in the spirit of appreciation and humility. From prayer to study, we give thanks for all we are receiving and for all the work He has done.

We must evaluate ourselves and examine areas where we exhibit the fruits of the flesh (**Galatians 5**). Take inventory of idols, emotions, and inclinations, then bring them to Jesus. Keep your eyes on Him, and He will begin to work them out.

Pride, outbursts of anger, enmity, disputes, sensuality, idolatry — any of these negative emotions are doorways for darkness and deception to have power in your life. We must pray through these issues. Ask Jesus to remove these influences, and He will teach you how to bring them under control. Not all at once, but one by one, these strongholds will be broken. He will give you knowledge through the Word and the wisdom to apply it through prayer.

You will stumble, but He will be there with grace upon grace. Your faith will grow stronger each time you recover. Through these trials, your understanding of the schemes of the world and the power of the Lord will deepen.

As you grow in your relationship, the strongholds of the old self are dismantled, and you begin to be hard-wired in the Spirit. Your struggle becomes victory; your innocence becomes maturity.

Perseverance is a key factor, and the key to perseverance is reading the Word and staying in prayer. There may be times when it feels like you are going through it alone, but He is never away from you. He strengthens your faith through your obedience. You will begin to hear the whisper of the Holy Spirit more clearly over time. After you have gained control over an emotion of the flesh, you will start to perceive more and more of the proofs of His existence in your life and the power of His will against any who come against it.

Proverbs 11:2

"When pride comes, then comes dishonor, but with the humble is wisdom."

Pride is a common starting point for Him to begin His work in you. In the pursuit of knowledge, the prideful lack the ability to accept instruction because they place themselves above God. Pride, vanity, and anger are all of the same cloth — hurdles that must be removed. We must get over ourselves so that He may work. Until we do,

His plan is obscured by our own plans, and our will is confused with His will. He pointed me to the Book of Ecclesiastes to help me understand anger and pride. Solomon writes through the lens of a world without God, where all of man's pursuits are pointless — a bunch of vain knuckleheads chasing the wind and stumbling through life because there is nothing better to do.

It hits too close to home for the unbeliever and exposes the foolishness of our past way of thinking.

You will see many ideas repeated throughout this work, one of them being that we are in a relationship of exchange. For everything we give up, we receive something better. In exchange for our pride, He gives humility and glory. In exchange for vanity, He gives modesty and unselfishness. In exchange for anger, we receive patience, peace, and comfort. These trade-offs cannot be perceived by the natural man, but to the spiritual man, these treasures are priceless.

Isaiah 1:19

"If you are willing and obedient, you shall eat the good of the land."

We are tempted by the thoughts of the old self. Lustful thoughts can lead us back to places, actions, or habits that once enslaved us in ignorance. Old habitual actions and emotions that bear the fruit of fear or anxiety in others must be recognized and dealt with through the power of Jesus, who is in us. If we impact those close to us with any emotions other than love, compassion, kindness, empathy, grace, or acceptance — anything of the Holy Spirit — it is contrary to what we are learning in our walk. Any toleration of such behavior will lead to enduring the lesson's conviction more than once.

It is easy to stumble in the beginning. Some issues take longer than others. Ghosts of old behavior, mental muscle memory, and habits formed in compliance with the world can make things difficult. The beauty of it is that the more you overcome your thoughts and urges, the more you desire obedience. The easier it becomes to rise above any issue or temptation that leads to the flesh. You will naturally start to avoid situations that may trigger your flesh. You will develop the ability to discern darkness around you and receive instruction on how to proceed. You will become more aware of yourself in relation to others and to God. Your eyes will see more, your ears will hear more.

The farther you advance in obedience, the easier it becomes to obey. The easier it is to obey, the more your spiritual gifts grow. The more you grow in your gifts, the stronger your faith becomes. All of these things build confidence; confidence leads to identity, and identity leads to dominion.

It is the beautiful cycle of life through the work of the Father, Son, and Holy Spirit. It is the mystery of God unfolding in our lives so that we may know eternal love and peace. His grace allows us to grasp His presence and experience a walk that we could never conceive as possible outside of Him because it is impossible to understand without Him.

Colossians 2:6

"Therefore, as you have received Christ Jesus the Lord, so walk in Him."

Deuteronomy 5:33

"You shall walk entirely in the way which the Lord your God has commanded you, so that you may live and that it may be well with you, and that you may prolong your days in the land which you will possess."

THE WAR FOR THE MIND

1 John 5:19

"We know that we are of God, and that the whole world lies in the power of the evil one."

We all must work out our own salvation. This is between you and Christ. My hope is, at this point in the walk — of which there is no time frame — that Jesus has been accepted into our hearts, that sinful ways have been repented of, and that we are striving to walk in obedience by staying in daily prayer with an appreciative heart, and by reading His Word to gain the knowledge required to understand the revelations He has for you: how to use the wisdom gifted to you and understand His plans for a future of peace and hope (**Jeremiah 29:11**).

The power in our spirit is greater than that of the world, but the power of the world is greater than that of our flesh. Our flesh is of the world, so it is under the power of the evil one. The devil takes a seat in your mind to influence you away from God. If your mind is breached, your heart can come under attack.

Think of your mind as a door to the Heavenly realm. While it resides in the world and can manifest the will of the flesh, it is also capable of manifesting the will of the Spirit. If we walk in the Spirit, through a personal relationship with Jesus, we can overcome the schemes of the world and live in a way that purifies the heart. On the other hand, if our spirit is aligned with the lies and false teachings of the physical realm, we will not overcome the adversary, and our spirit will be enslaved by the sin of our flesh. We will spend our existence in bondage because we chose not to accept the teachings of Christ or the grace of the God of Peace. Instead, we chose human understanding, to be dragged into the pit of unforgiveness and regret; we chose to stand alone and were swept away by the deceptions of the devil.

Let us dive into some of these deceptions. Many are apparent, but as you go through the refining process, you will discern many that may surprise you. Your mind will be opened to more and more of Satan's nuances and subtleties as you walk deeper in the Spirit. You will understand firsthand how he infects your heart by manipulating your mind.

Romans 16:17-18

"(17) Now I urge you, brethren, keep your eye on those who cause dissension and hindrances contrary to the teaching which you have learned, and turn away from them.

(18) For such men are slaves, not of the Lord Christ, but of their own appetites; and by their smooth and flattering speech they deceive the hearts of the unsuspecting."

The devil infects the masses easily through manipulation by leaders — from the top to the bottom. Politicians that write laws contrary to God's will deliver the nation and its society directly into darkness. We must realize what stems from the politics of man to see the many entry points of darkness that can work against your spirit.

Power, greed, lies, and manipulation run rampant in the upper crust; anger, hate, judgment, pride, and disdain for others are the scourge of the layman. All of the arguing and distraction is poison from the serpent to weaken us spiritually and keep us divided. Teachers and scientists often bring forward theories of the physical world and teach them as fact, while ignoring the truth of God and mocking the spiritual.

The natural man labels the path to love and peace as superstition or mythology and sees the mythological as lunacy. Preachers and denominational worship are not immune to the desires of the flesh. Satan disguises himself as an angel of light. The adversary knows Scripture better than any man and will speak in truths, half-truths, and lies mixed in so that the full truth is never perceived until you accept Christ. This is why we must discern everything through prayer and Scripture so that we shall not be deceived.

Please do not misunderstand me; I am not saying all churches are bad. The Spirit will give you eyes to see and ears to hear so that you may discern your setting. Do not fear churches, but in all things, guard your mind and protect your heart. In the beginning, focus more on your personal walk with Jesus than on what is going on at church. Until you are strong enough in the Spirit to repel the fiery darts of the self-righteous and judgmental, keep your eyes on Him or pray for thick skin. Stay focused on establishing yourself with Jesus. He gives us understanding individually through prayer and the Word. He saves us one at a time, so let no person or group come between you and your salvation.

While there is a remnant of Spirit-filled, Word-led churches, they are the exception, not the rule. By the math Jesus used when He spoke of the churches in the Book of Revelation (chapters 1-3), six of the seven churches will be led astray. Preachers and priests can stumble when the desires of the flesh override the desires of the Spirit. Anyone who stands with God becomes an enemy to the flesh and a target for attack, especially those spreading truth and peace.

When they stumble, the devil is there in a heartbeat to sell them anything but freedom. Whatever is useful to him will be used to manipulate your mind until it infects your heart. An infected heart becomes hardened, and a hardened heart cannot hear God.

Local clubs and organizations can also lead members astray. If we cling to ideas or activities contrary to what we have learned from Him, we allow the world a foothold in our minds, leading to darkness, idolatry, and other strongholds that must eventually be refined.

Ephesians 2:2

"The devil is the prince of the power of the air, working in the sons of disobedience."

Let us be discerning in all our media pursuits. Those twinges in your spirit when you scroll past anger, hate, or division are the adversary pulling his chair away from the table of your mind so that he may take his seat. We must cast away such intrusions, for they have no value. We must put aside the things that darken our eyes.

Luke 11:34

"The lamp of your body is your eye; when your eye is clear, your whole body is also full of light; but when it is bad, your body also is full of darkness."

These are all outside influences designed to numb the spirit and empower the flesh. They create a habitat for internal darkness to flourish, which must be refined for us to understand the love and peace of God. This darkness can build slowly through sin — a chance outburst or a grudge can grow into a stronghold — or it can originate from physically or mentally traumatic experiences, which can create lifelong strongholds immediately. Trauma can lead to many fruits of the flesh, with anger and pride being some of the most common today.

Dogmas from false teachings, hate, and an ungodly upbringing; loss, regret, and unforgiveness — all these can easily become demonic strongholds. In our transformation, we must assail these strongholds to burn off the flesh.

Joshua 1:9

"Have I not commanded you? Be strong and courageous! Do not be afraid nor be dismayed, for the Lord your God is with you wherever you go."

If you give your pride to the Lord, He will give you glory. If you give your lust to the Lord, He will give you self-control. If you give your regret to the Lord, He will give you contentment. If you give your anger to the Lord, He will give you peace. And do not forget forgiveness. He has forgiven us so that we may have no unforgiveness in our hearts. Unforgiveness hardens the heart and steals joy. He expects us to forgive others and ourselves. Do not carry unforgiveness any longer than necessary. Ask the Lord to take it from you, and He will start the process. His exchange rate is unmatched, and the results are undeniable if given time to complete the refinements.

We see how stumbling blocks exist in almost every aspect of our lives. Jesus teaches us to understand these situations and motives while showing us how to be the gatekeepers of our minds. We must keep our eyes on Him so that our spiritual path is not darkened. Every thought and emotion planted by the enemy must be taken to Jesus and removed. Crush the seeds planted by the ruler of the world, or they will produce fruits of death.

Psalm 25:15

"My eyes are ever toward the Lord, for He shall pluck my feet out of the net."

PRAY DAILY

Earlier we mentioned the importance of perseverance. We cannot persevere on our own, but only through prayer and the Word of Jesus Christ. The devil uses the spirit of religion to deceive many on this point. He would have us believe that we must enter into Christ through man, that salvation can only be had through an anointed leader in a building of worship. This is simply not true. The Lord says that none shall slip through His hands. All of God's children will have the chance to receive His gift of grace, and not all men have access to a holy man or a holy structure. Remember that Christ is in us; our relationship is personal, and nothing is out of reach for Him.

Finding a good worship building can go a long way in our growth through encouragement, fellowship, and the testimony of others. When you are spending time there, it is time spent with your eyes on

Him. This is a habit to develop so that your eyes are not on the world. Know that the most important thing you can do is abide in Him, stay in His Word, place everything before Him in prayer, and He will show you truth from lies so that nothing may come between you and the Spirit.

Let us not be content merely with the warmth from the Spirit of the congregation or the preacher. While it may be comforting to sit in the glow of another's fire, it falls short of His plan. His expectation is that we make our own fire, with Him, in our secret place, so that we may bring warmth to the congregation. Edify the body of Christ so that the world can see the proofs of His work in us, so that our true identity may be known to the world to serve His purpose.

Secret Place – Psalm 91:1

"He who dwells in the secret place of the Most High shall abide under the shadow of the Almighty."

I mention the secret place — the place where we commune with Him, the place where mysteries are revealed. It is our shelter where we can be still outside of the storm, where the work of God is written on our hearts, and where we build our relationship through open dialogue. Here, we can bring our appreciation, our prayers — anything and everything should be put before Him in this place.

Matthew 6:6

"But you, when you pray, go into your room, and when you have shut your door, pray to your Father who is in the secret place; and your Father who sees in secret will reward you openly."

How to Approach Prayer

There are miles of commentary on prayer — how to pray, where to pray, what to pray, and when to pray — but let us not complicate the process. Prayer is personal; it is the time to be truthful so that what lies within is brought to light and pulled up by its roots. His desire is that you seek Him, and in His joy, we are transformed. The way you communicate with Him develops as your relationship deepens.

Let us note two verses that shape the nature of our prayer:

1 John 5:14

"Now this is the confidence that we have in Him, that if we ask anything according to His will, He will hear us."

We see that if we pray for our development and transformation according to His will, our prayers will be heard. If we pray for things outside His will, we should not expect a response. We must be self-aware enough to know when we are getting in the way of His work by our own understanding or will. Our best-laid plans fall short of understanding. We must embrace Him with faith and confidence so that it becomes natural to submit to His plan.

James 4:3

"You ask and do not receive, because you ask with wrong motives, so that you may spend it on your pleasures."

Here, James tells us that if we are not praying in the heart of the Spirit, we will be denied what we ask for. Wrong motives are the motives of the flesh or those that might lead to the manifestation of the flesh. Let us make sure our hearts are in the right place. Remember Solomon, who was granted anything he wanted, and he chose wisdom. Through wisdom comes everything else.

Colossians 4:2

"Devote yourselves to prayer, keeping alert in it, with an attitude of thanksgiving."

As we leave old ways behind, we replace them with the habits of the new man. The two most important habits to develop are prayer and reading His Word. These things should be done daily. If you are struggling to pray daily, tell Him that. He appreciates honesty.

There were many days early in my walk when my prayer consisted of:

"Dear Jesus, here I am. I am struggling with prayer. Please help me so that I may have more to say tomorrow. Amen."

In the beginning, it goes a long way just to check in. Remember, you are starting the process of hard-wiring yourself into the Spirit. Like many other things in your relationship, these habits are harder at first, but as you gain momentum, they will be written on your heart, and you will long to speak with Him about everything.

Romans 12:12

"Rejoicing in hope, patient in tribulation, continuing steadfastly in prayer."

- Rejoice in your faith and the hope He has promised.
- Patience is required to persevere through our renewal and tribulation.

Anxiety, worry, and doubt are common schemes of the devil. The adversary wants to keep you in the flesh and will use any emotion to set you back. Recognize these as tricks designed to throw you off the path. He will teach you to overcome all that comes against you in the world by first overcoming yourself so that you may be prepared.

1 Thessalonians 5:16-18

(16) Rejoice always;

(17) pray without ceasing;

(18) in everything give thanks; for this is God's will for you in Christ Jesus."

As you develop your prayer habit, you will find yourself going to Him constantly throughout the day. You will become more engaged as you see His proofs in you.

- Show appreciation in all your prayers. Personally, I start every prayer by addressing Jesus and giving thanks for all He has done for me, for all His creation, gifts, grace, patience, and love.

- Then I pray for repentance and forgiveness so that I may be clean while I speak with Him.
- Talk to Him like a friend. Pray for others, pray for His will, pray that you may see His will, that you may receive the gifts according to His grace, and always pray for understanding, discernment, and wisdom — for He freely gives.
- Pray as if you have already received these things from Him. Be humble before Him and always be thankful.

Mark 11:24

"Therefore I say to you, all things for which you pray and ask, believe that you have received them, and they will be granted to you."

Speak To God. Pray Daily.

THE WORD

John 1:1-2

(1) In the beginning was the Word, and the Word was with God, and the Word was God.

(2) He was in the beginning with God.

Do you find it curious that God made light on day one, vegetation on day three, and the sun on day four? Jesus is the light from the beginning; the Spirit of God was moving over the surface of the waters. God spoke all things into existence.

YHWH is so loving that He gave us three manifestations so that we may have all that we need to prepare for judgment day. Jesus is our advocate, our access to the gifts of God. Through the Word, we have access to direct knowledge from God. Through the Holy Spirit, we receive the understanding we need to complete the picture, to complete our obedience.

The answers you seek to the mysteries of the universe cannot be found in the wisdom of men, but only through the understanding of God. The truth is available to us, but we have forgotten where to find it. The world buries it deep under the drama of mankind—an invaluable treasure hidden in hopes that it may never be found, for the Prince of this world understands its dominion and power.

Can we not see that the very thing that drives us to search for the truth, the very thing that tells us something is off, the very thing that stirs up our rebellion against "man," was put there by God? Not so that we would rebel against our governing bodies, but so that we would turn away from the schemes of man. It was put there by the Almighty so that we would know, in our inner being, that we are being deceived by the adversary and that we do not have to be content living in a lie.

2 Timothy 3:16-17

(16) All scripture is inspired by God and profitable for teaching, for reproof, for correction, for training in righteousness;

(17) so that the man of God may be adequate, equipped for every good work.

I would like to take a moment to address a bit of nonsense that makes its way around both secular and religious circles.

An argument fueled by those who lack understanding, those without ears to hear or eyes to see.

If you are hung up on the writings of fallible men, then rejoice, for it is proof that the Lord uses fallible men! Amen! If not, what purpose would we have other than arguing over nonsensical subjects designed to separate us from the truth and achieve the very purpose of division?

ALL SCRIPTURE IS INSPIRED BY GOD! And when you realize this simple truth, He will develop in you the understanding of the inspiration of God. He gives proofs of His work to those who walk with Him.

If you are hung up on interpretations, you are firmly in the grasp of the devil. I went down this trail until I realized it was feeding my fear, not my faith—fruits of the flesh be gone!

Personally, I searched for the best word-for-word translation and was pointed to the NASB. I do the majority of my reading and study through this translation, and I have grown leaps and bounds in my relationship with Him. I have also been reading the New King James, and the growth of my walk has not diminished.

My revelations are only information to anyone else, but I can promise you that they can lead to an existence completely outside the realm of understanding you have right now. My view from my current vantage point would have seemed unimaginable when I started this walk. I find myself thanking Him 20 times a day because His ways are so crazy. Well, His ways are different from our ways; I can only imagine how crazy our ways are to Him. He backs up the promises He makes in the Bible—the same promises that are scoffed at by a world that offers nothing, no hope, no love. Look around: we have people going hungry and without shelter; the world does not care—it is part of its fruits. Through the understanding of God's love, we can also love. We learn to refrain from the pointless arguing with one another about who has love, who is being loved, and who is not getting any love. If we would concentrate on the Word and live by the wisdom of the Word, all the love the world needs would come naturally, with no dispute.

Billy Graham was a spiritual powerhouse— did he receive his understanding through the King James Version? Very likely. Whichever interpretation he used was righteous indeed. I know many young people who may use the ESV or NASB, and they are walking with the Spirit.

My point is that the power is not in the translation; it is in the Word of God. I pray all people see through the lies that keep us away from our true identity.

The Word will renew your mind and soften your heart. You will find that sitting down in your quiet place and reading the Word is not a chore, as it may seem to the followers of religion, but a spiritual meeting with God. The more you walk in the Spirit, the more you crave these times—excited for what He has next, thankful for all that He has shown you. Each time you sit down, try to do so with humility and appreciation. You will grow in respect and reverence for your Creator the more time you spend with Him.

As with any part of building this relationship, these things do not happen overnight. Remember that we are rewiring the brain in the new man, building the habits we need to overcome the world. I would like to add the importance of studying out of an actual Bible. Bible apps are good for quick reference or comparing verses in different translations—that is fine. When it comes down to the daily reading of the Word, remember that God is in that physical book, completely unhindered, ready to come alive in your hands and eager to share His secrets. Maybe it's the union of physical touch and metaphysical communion that sparks the power of the relationship. It is still a mystery to me, but I know that when I am holding and reading His book, He is well pleased.

If you do not feel like it, or you are struggling in the beginning—which you will, everyone does—be honest with Him. Tell Him, *"Lord, I am having trouble reading this morning; help me to overcome the old man so that I may be hungry for Your Word tomorrow."* Open your Bible to a random page and read a single verse. Through this simple action, you are watering the seed so that He can work. You are establishing the habit of picking up your Bible and reading at least one verse every day, and the payoff will astound you.

Remember, anyone who is quick to argue or carries strife or division is not of Christ, for these are tools of the devil and spread darkness. God wants us to unite in love, not be divided or darkened by senseless exchanges that do nothing for the kingdom of heaven.

Matthew 4:4

But He answered and said, "It is written, 'Man shall not live on bread alone, but on every word that proceeds out of the mouth of God.'"

Do we not feed the natural man bread so that he can sustain? Then why must we insist on starving our spirit? If we starve our spirit, it becomes all the more difficult to hear the voice of God. When we deny our Spirit the nourishment of the Word of God, we are ignoring the most powerful part of our whole being. Without the Word, there is no growth in Christ. Where there is no growth in Christ, there is a man walking in the flesh. Where there is a man walking in the flesh—well, **DEAD MAN WALKING!** Zombies on Earth? Why yes, we are surrounded.

The Spirit is sustained by every word that proceeds out of the mouth of God, which was written down, collected, and translated through inspiration given by God. Man alone does not have the capacity to accomplish this. The proof is evident in all other works written by man; there is only **one living Word.** Dead works are the construct of man; inspiration is the construct of God.

Hebrews 4:12

For the word of God is living and powerful, and sharper than any two-edged sword, piercing even to the division of soul and spirit, of joints and marrow, and is a discerner of the thoughts and intents of the heart.

You will hear many times the phrase that the Word is the living Word. This is another one of the many proofs He gives to His believers. Let us first establish that we seek truth from a living God, and through the resurrection of Christ, He is alive in us. If they were the words of a dead prophet who followed a dead god, then the power of the words would also be dead, and nothing would be alive in you but the spirit of antichrist.

The living Word means that the Word is alive in your life. You may read a verse at the beginning of your walk and take understanding from it. Then you may read it again a year later, and it gives you a new understanding that is always in line with the previous one but serves to pull back the curtain just a little more. Maybe the wisdom you receive is the answer to problems or issues in your life. His ways are not our ways, and His ways transcend our wildest imaginations.

2 Corinthians 3:2

You are our letter, written in our hearts, known and read by all men;

I share one more verse and one more nugget of understanding He has shown to me.

Through the covenant of grace, the Word was written on our hearts. When we come to Christ, our hearts are hardened and dirty. As we abide in Him, through daily prayer and reading the Word, our hearts soften. We start to wipe away the dirt and reveal the Word written underneath. Each time you glean something new from a scripture, it is because, through His inexpressible grace, love, and patience, there has been cleansing in that spot since the last time you read that scripture.

Let God speak to you—open your Bible daily.

EMBRACE YOUR WALK IN THE SPIRIT

Matthew 18:1-4

(1) At that time the disciples came to Jesus, saying, "Who then is greatest in the kingdom of heaven?"

(2) And He called a child to Himself and set him before them,

(3) and said, "Truly I say to you, unless you are converted and become like children, you shall not enter the kingdom of heaven."

(4) "Whoever humbles himself as this child, he is the greatest in the kingdom of heaven."

Look, I know this is hard to see and harder to imagine, but in this relationship with Christ we become as children to the Father. His work in our lives leaves us with childlike wonderment. Through the direct teaching of Jesus and through walking in the Holy Spirit, letting Him guide you, you will be transformed beyond any concept of God you may have at this time. Your future understanding will be greater than your current imagination.

I implore you to read Paul's letters, and the teachings of Jesus in the Gospels of Matthew, Mark, Luke, and John. Imagine, if you will, all the peace, love, and transformation that is written there—imagine it as fact. Try to picture life through the lens of Jesus and what that world would look like. That is the true possibility of your existence. Your true identity lies in Him. To know this place, you only have to accept Jesus into your heart with humility and thanksgiving, to allow yourself to be refined, and to allow your mind to be renewed. Everything He speaks is real and is actively being revealed to you.

Why must we insist on living in the past, carrying the baggage of our mistakes, and being enslaved by darkness? Our arrogance and pride will be our destruction. The devil has turned our existence into a dystopian romance, where, in the end, man will overcome. Man can never overcome the forces of darkness alone. We must have the correct spiritual training; we must have Jesus in us. Spirit defeats spirit while the flesh rots away.

Our society has adopted the mindset that our darkness defines us, that our identity may be established through the victim we claim to be, that we are made known in death, not in life. You will come to realize that what is considered a necessity in the world is the complete opposite of what Jesus teaches us. Turn away from the lies of the flesh.

Your true walk with Christ will mean that He is working through you. The people around you will feel His presence through your obedience to Him. Gone will be the anger and rage that defined you—those feelings from the adversary that you gave to Jesus, exchanged for love, peace, and true understanding. The ways you repented from will no longer belittle you, and through your new ways, Christ will elevate and empower you.

I pray that everyone who reads this comes into a personal relationship with Jesus Christ, so that we all may know the truth. The path I have outlined has changed my life beyond anything I could have dreamed. The amazing thing is: it is all written in black and white, a myriad of layers that give life to the dead, called the Bible.

The Lord's Prayer — Matthew 6:9-13

(9) "Pray then in this way: 'Our Father which art in heaven, hallowed be thy name,

(10) Thy kingdom come, thy will be done in earth, as it is in heaven,

(11) Give us this day our daily bread,

(12) And forgive us our trespasses, as we forgive those that trespass against us,

(13) And lead us not into temptation, but deliver us from evil; for thine is the kingdom, and the power, and the glory forever. Amen.'"

ACCEPTANCE PRAYER

Dear Heavenly Father,

I know that I am a sinner and I ask for your forgiveness.

I believe you died for my sins and rose from the dead.

I turn from my sins, I repent of my sins;

I invite you to come into my heart and life.

I want to trust and follow you as my Lord and Savior,

In Jesus name, Amen.